How To...

PLAY BLUES PIANO BY EAR

BY TODD LOWRY

7777 W. BLUEMOUND RD. P.O. BOX 13819 MILWAUKEE, WI 53213

ISBN 978-1-4803-5315-2

In Australia Contact:
Hal Leonard Australia Pty. Ltd.
4 Lentara Court
Cheltenham, Victoria, 3192 Australia
Email: ausadmin@halleonard.com.au

Visit Hal Leonard Online at
www.halleonard.com

CONTENTS

4	Introduction
5	Chapter 1: What Is Blues Piano?
6	Chapter 2: What Is Playing by Ear?
7	Chapter 3: Mental Approach to Playing by Ear
8	Chapter 4: Posture, Hand Position, & Finger Numbers
10	Chapter 5: How to Practice
11	Chapter 6: The Musical Alphabet & the Piano Keyboard
13	Chapter 7: Basic Chords
15	Chapter 8: The 12-Bar Blues Progression
18	Chapter 9: The Basic Left-Hand Pattern
23	Chapter 10: Right-Hand Improvisation Using the Blues Scales
26	Chapter 11: Blues in G
29	Chapter 12: Special Blues Techniques
34	Chapter 13: Straight-Eighth-Note Blues
36	Chapter 14: Early Rock-and-Roll
40	Chapter 15: Gospel Blues
42	Chapter 16: Boogie Woogie
44	Chapter 17: Other Blues Styles
49	Chapter 18: Using Tritones
53	Chapter 19: Blues Intros & Endings
56	Chapter 20: Once More, with Feeling
57	Chapter 21: Playing in a Blues Band
58	Chapter 22: Improvisation Ideas
59	Play-Along Tracks
60	Appendix I: A Brief History of Blues Piano
63	Appendix II: Blues Piano Players

INTRODUCTION

How to Play Blues Piano by Ear aims to teach you how to sit down at the piano and play blues with both hands – with no note-reading skills whatsoever. Its contents apply to any acoustic piano, digital piano, or electronic keyboard.

The book is tailored for anyone who wants to learn to play blues piano by ear, including: beginners who have never played the piano at all; those who took piano lessons earlier in their lives, but have since lapsed; and those who are able to play music "by the note," but want also to be able to play blues piano without relying on sheet music.

All musical examples are shown by piano keyboard diagrams, so it is assumed that you know – or will immediately learn – the names of the notes and their position on the keyboard. That information is contained herein, but no note reading is necessary.

ABOUT THE ONLINE AUDIO

The price of this book includes access to audio tracks online, for download or streaming, using the unique code on the title page. The tracks provide an audio demonstration of each example in the book, performed by the author. For your personal practice, additional play-along tracks – a professional band performing blues numbers in various styles – are included.

CHAPTER 1
WHAT IS BLUES PIANO?

The blues had its origin in the call-and-response patterns of African tribal music. Its evolution continued in the field hollers and spirituals of black slaves in 18th and 19th century America.

Blues piano styles had their origin in the rough-and-tumble barrelhouses of the railroad, lumber, and turpentine camps in Louisiana and East Texas in the late 1800s and early 1900s. There, itinerant pianists developed a style that had enough rhythmic thrust and was aggressive enough to be heard above the crowd and to keep up with the rowdy atmosphere.

Often, piano players were imitating the trains that ran from camp to camp. A rhythmic bass chugged along and train-like whistles rang out in the upper right hand. This pounding style became known as "barrelhouse" piano. The boogie-woogie piano style developed out of the same factors. Eventually, the blues moved up the Mississippi from New Orleans to St. Louis, Kansas City, Chicago, and beyond.

Blues pianists began to gain popularity in the 1920s. The boogie-woogie styles became a foundation of big-band swing and jazz in the 1930s. Jump blues (a fast, frolicking style of blues) became very popular in the 1940s. In the 1950s, rock-and-roll developed straight out of blues piano, with the main pioneers being Jerry Lee Lewis and Johnnie Johnson (Chuck Berry's pianist). At the same time, blues pianists Ray Charles and Fats Domino created R&B and soul music.

In the history of American music, the importance of the blues cannot be overestimated. Its spirit and flavor pervade all jazz. The effect of the blues can be clearly felt in rock, country, R&B, and pop. Although the term "blues" connotes melancholy or lament, the spirit of the blues is often something else. The blues is frequently played with great rhythmic vitality. Many times it sounds joyous and life-affirming.

This book will get you started playing authentic blues, even if you are a total beginner.

CHAPTER 2
WHAT IS PLAYING BY EAR?

Myth: Music made by ear is inferior to music made by reading exactly what's on the page.

Fact: Playing by ear is actually the most natural way to make music.

Long before music notation was developed in ancient Greece, people created and preserved music, using only their ears and memories. Music is an aural art. Ultimately, the ear guides all playing. All folk music traditions are handed down aurally, by ear.

Many well-known tunesmiths don't read a note of music. For example, Irving Berlin had only a few years of schooling, could not read music, was self-taught on the piano, and played the piano using only the black keys. Nevertheless, he managed to write thousands of songs, including "White Christmas" and "God Bless America." A host of other great songwriters cannot notate their own tunes. So how did they learn music? They picked it up in the same way we master speech – by the imitation and repetition of sounds.

Here's another little-known fact: Popular sheet music is typically created by a transcriber only after a song becomes a hit. In fact, I used to be on staff at the world's largest music publisher. My job was to listen to popular recordings and write out the songs in musical notation for sale as sheet music.

Myth: Some people are tone-deaf.

Fact: There is no such thing as tone-deafness. People who believe they are tone-deaf simply have underdeveloped pitch-matching ability. Like any skill, this is learned through practice. If a person were actually tone-deaf, he or she wouldn't be able to distinguish one song from another.

Myth: To play by ear requires a special, inborn talent.

Fact: There is nothing magical about playing by ear. I know many pianists trained in the classical manner who insist they cannot improvise or play by ear. However, when a pianist says he cannot improvise or play by ear, he is merely saying that he is reluctant to try playing by ear. Fear and inhibition are the only obstacles.

Learning to play piano is basically a self-taught process. No matter how many lessons or classes you take, results come from practicing and working things out on your own. Playing by ear at the piano is easier than most people expect it to be. Of course, some instruction is needed and this book is intended to supply just that.

CHAPTER 3
MENTAL APPROACH TO PLAYING BY EAR

Instead of "play by ear," musicians often say "jam," "ad-lib," or "improvise." Regardless of the term used, this should be part of every musician's development. Learning to play blues piano by ear is a two-step process. First, you must acquire the basic musical vocabulary of blues piano music. Secondly, you must spend time practicing at the piano to develop your skills.

If you are one the kind of person who is used to playing strictly from the written score, you may feel awkward at first. You may think your ideas are not good or that you'll never "get it." When this happens, just keep going. Playing blues is learned by doing and it doesn't come instantly. It takes time, so keep practicing.

Do you remember your first experience of riding a bike or snow-skiing or ice-skating? When you fell down, you got back up again. Soon, with a little more practice, you weren't falling down as often. With enough practice, you didn't fall down at all.

Playing blues is like that. It's learned by doing. You have to expect to make mistakes. Proficiency comes though practice. Don't be afraid of not knowing where your next step will land. Eventually, your confidence in your playing will grow along with your abilities. The ultimate goal is to be able to blend musical elements with your own imagination in order for you to improvise blues spontaneously.

We need to shed negative attitudes that inhibit us. A musician, like an athlete, cannot perform to his potential if he is constantly questioning his own abilities. Everyone has creative ability that can be activated and nurtured. Playing by ear is natural and intuitive. It involves "letting go" and not worrying about making mistakes. In fact, mistakes are good. In his book *Themes and Conclusions*, the great Russian composer Igor Stravinsky wrote, "I learned more through my mistakes and pursuits of false assumptions than from my exposure to founts of wisdom and knowledge."

Improvisation is something that is learned. Note that we call performing on the piano "playing the piano." "Play" indicates that it is supposed to be fun, that it is something to be done for its own sake, for the joy of it.

Other useful approaches to learning to playing blues by ear include:

- Listening to blues music to subconsciously assimilate its nature.

- Practicing technical exercises such as scales and broken chords to develop facility at the keyboard.

- Learning blues compositions from the printed sources that are available.

Playing the blues can be a lifetime pursuit. This book is just a starting point. Study blues pianists. Make use of books, CDs, DVDs, and online resources. Most of the examples in this book are written in the key of C or G, but you should learn blues in several keys.

A few more thoughts on improvising:

- Each student learns in a different way. Just as there are many paths up any mountain peak, there are several paths to the same goal.

- Improvisation is fun. Do it for the fun of it.

- Improvise every day.

CHAPTER 4

POSTURE, HAND POSITION, & FINGER NUMBERS

POSTURE

No two pianists look alike at the piano. Some pianists barely move while playing. Others, such as Keith Jarrett, undulate and writhe constantly. The important thing is to feel comfortable and relaxed. Sit facing the middle of the keyboard. Set the chair or bench at a distance from the piano that is to your own liking. Adjust the height so that your elbows are on the same level as the keyboard.

HAND POSITION

Allow the upper arm to hang loosely, with the forearm, wrist, and hand in line with the keyboard. Your hands assume a shape as if holding a small round object, such as an orange or tennis ball, from above.

Curve your fingers gently, with the fleshy part (not the nails) touching the keys. The side of the thumb touches the keys. Let the natural position of your hands determine which part of the key you depress with the tip of the finger.

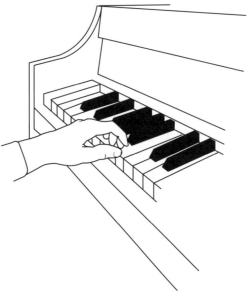

FINGER NUMBERS

In piano sheet music, fingering is often written out above or below the notes in small numerals. Each thumb is numbered 1, the index fingers are 2, the middle fingers 3, the ring fingers 4, and the pinkie fingers 5. Printed fingering is simply a suggestion given by an editor. Do not hesitate to alter it. Appropriate fingering is one that works for you and that feels comfortable and natural.

Though we won't be reading sheet music, for our purposes here, we need to know the finger numbers.

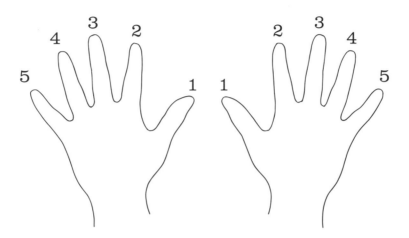

Finding the right fingering for a musical passage requires a little thought and experimentation. When learning to play any piece of music, decide on a consistent fingering and write it down. This will save you time and frustration in the long run, and will make passages easier to play.

WARNING SIGNS

Musicians are like athletes. While sports that require running, throwing, or kicking tax the big muscles of the body, the piano makes extreme demands on small muscles. Pain in the fingers, wrists, or arms is an indication that you are either overusing the muscles, using the wrong muscles, or playing with too much tension. It is a sign to relax and slow down.

CHAPTER 5
HOW TO PRACTICE

Practice is the only way to improve on the piano. Practice, practice, practice. This requires time, effort and discipline. However, practice does not have to be drudgery, and what you put into music will pay you back many times over. The following suggestions are aimed at helping you achieve enjoyable, productive practice sessions.

- Relax. Try a few shoulder rolls to get rid of stress in your neck and shoulders. Gently shake out your hands to get the blood flowing. If they are cold, run them under warm water for a minute or two. Also, a few deep breaths will help you relax and focus your mind.

- Regular daily practice, even for as little as 20 minutes, is better than playing for several hours once or twice a week. The quality of practice is more important than the time spent. Choose times when you can relax and be on your own – and not be stressed out, distracted, or interrupted. Practice in physically pleasant surroundings.

- Practice should be conscious, not mechanical. While it's good to learn your scales, arpeggios, and chords, do not play like a robot.

- Practice with a plan and with specific goals in mind. What do you wish to accomplish today? Are you trying to learn new song? Are you striving to tighten up a tune you've been working on? Play it until you've "got it." When you come back to it, recall what you did before. Build on what you've already done.

- Establish a comfortable fingering for each new piece.

- When learning a new song, there often seems to be too much happening at once. The best way to cope with a song's complexities is to disassemble it. Separate the two hands. Play each hand by itself.

- Identify the song's constituent parts. Some sections of the music are likely to be more difficult than others. Always practice the hard parts more than the easy parts.

- Slow it down. Be patient. Hard pieces or the hard parts of pieces become easier when played slowly. Also, you should slow down to cultivate evenness and smoothness in your playing. Start slowly and gradually work up to the proper speed. The goals of practice are smooth and even playing, playing at the correct speed, and playing expressively.

- Try recording your practice to evaluate whether your playing really sounds like you think it does. You may hear things (good or bad) that you're not really aware of. Keep your recordings and mark the date on them. If you ever feel like you are not progressing, go back and listen to an earlier session and see how much your playing has improved.

- Heighten your rhythmic sense by sometimes playing with a metronome. This will help develop more rhythmic accuracy and continuity.

- Don't overuse the sustain pedal.

- Take every opportunity to play with other musicians, singers, friends, and family. Music is expression meant to be shared. Learn to jam with others.

- Listen to recorded piano performances. Attend live performances.

- It's useful to memorize pieces. People do this in different ways. It's better to have music memory (aural) than just "finger memory," which is acquired from repetition and is your fingers working mechanically.

- Never say, "I can't do it." Instead, say, "I haven't done it *yet*."

CHAPTER 6
THE MUSICAL ALPHABET
& THE PIANO KEYBOARD

The fundamental frequency – in other words, the "highness" or "lowness" – of a tone is called its pitch. Moving to the right on the keyboard is "going up," causing a higher pitch. Moving to the left on the keyboard is "going down," causing a lower pitch.

The piano keyboard is arranged in a regular pattern of black and white keys. There are only seven letter names used in music: A, B, C, D, E, F, and G. These seven letter names repeat over and over again on the white keys of the keyboard. The distance from one pitch to the next pitch with the same letter name (either up or down) is called an "octave." The piano's range is more than seven octaves.

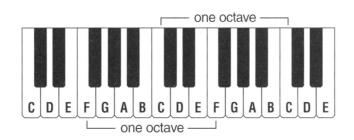

Look at the keyboard and count each group of black keys. Notice how they are arranged in groups of two black keys and three black keys. This pattern of twos and threes makes it easy for us to keep track of where we are on the keyboard.

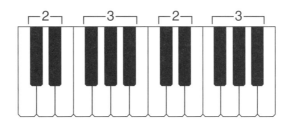

The white key to the left of every grouping of two black keys is called C. Middle C is the C closest to the middle of the keyboard.

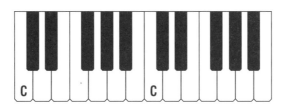

The white key to the left of every group of three black notes is called F.

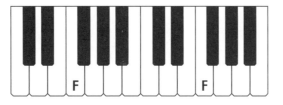

The black keys take their name from the adjacent white keys. Each black key has two names, either a flat or a sharp, depending on the context. A sharp is above (to the right of) a specific white key and a flat is below (to the left of) a specific white key. For instance, the black note to the right of middle C can be called C♯, because it's above the C; or we can refer to it as D♭ because it's directly below the D. The context and key generally determine whether the black note is called a flat or a sharp.

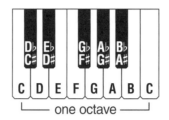

The distance between any two notes is called an "interval." The distance between any two adjacent keys (going up or going down) is called a "half step." It is the smallest interval used in Western music. The distance between B and C is a "half step." The distance between C and C♯ is also a half-step.

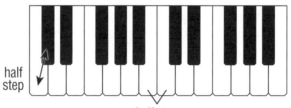

CHAPTER 7

BASIC CHORDS

Harmony is the art of combining notes into chords. A *chord* is a group of three or more notes played simultaneously. A *triad* is a three-note chord. Triads are the most basic chords. There are four basic kinds of triads: major, minor, diminished, and augmented. In this book, we will concern ourselves only with major and minor triads.

Chords take their name from the *root* of the chord. The root of a C major chord is C. The root of a C minor chord is also C. When the root of a chord is the lowest note in the chord the chord is said to be in *root position*. For the most part, we will use root-position chords.

CHORD FORMULAS

We find the other notes in a chord by counting up various numbers of half steps from the root. The formulas for major chords, minor chords, and 7th chords are as follows:

For a *major* chord, find the root, then count up four half steps for the second note; from there, count up three half steps for the third note. The formula is: root; up four half steps; up three half steps.

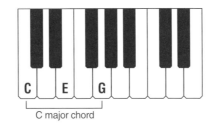

C major chord

For a *minor* chord, find the root, then count up three half steps for the second note; from there, count up four half steps for the third note. The formula is root; up three half steps; up four half steps.

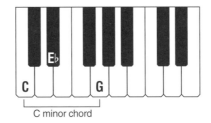

C minor chord

7TH CHORDS

The *7th chord* is an additional sonority we are going to use. A 7th chord – also called a *dominant 7th chord* (V7)– has four notes. It is formed adding another note to a major triad, three half steps above the triad's top note. Thus, the formula is: root; up four half steps; up three half steps; up three half steps.

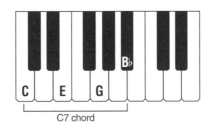

C7 chord

CHORD SYMBOLS

Popular music uses chord symbols as a method of abbreviating chord names.

    G   G7   C   G

A-mazing grace, how sweet the sound,

      Em   A7   D7

That saved a wretch like me!

Chord symbol names have two parts: the chord root and the chord suffix. The initial letter indicates the root of the chord, i.e. what note the chord is built upon. The suffix (made up of letters or numbers) tells you the chord type. Thus, a C minor chord is built on the root of C and is a minor-type chord.

The symbol for a major chord is a capital letter (the chord root). Thus, an F major chord is abbreviated simply as **F**. The symbol for a minor chord is a capital letter (the chord root) followed by a small letter "m" for minor. Thus, C minor is abbreviated as **Cm**. (Note: An old-fashioned way of indicating minor used a dash instead of the small m. Thus, C minor was indicated as **C-**. One sometimes encounters that notation, in publications such as the *Real Books*.) The symbol for a 7th chord is a capital letter (the root) followed by a 7: **C7** or **Cm7**, for example.

CHAPTER 8

THE 12-BAR BLUES PROGRESSION

The 12-bar blues progression is the most common of blues structures. In fact, it is the most frequently used structure in all of Western popular music, be it blues, rock, or jazz. It is at the root of every popular musical style of the 20th century, including jazz, rock, R&B, hip-hop, and country. The 12-bar blues form evolved in the Mississippi delta in the late 19th century as a synthesis of African and European musical elements.

Blues pervades all of jazz. When playing a jazz date with a jazz group, the leader of the group will often just say, "Let's a play a blues in F," and then count it off and all the musicians are expected to know what to do.

Nearly every great popular songwriter – including George Gershwin, Duke Ellington, Bob Dylan, John Lennon & Paul McCartney, and Hank Williams – wrote music that is blues or blues-based. Likewise, the 12-bar blues progression is the foundation of boogie-woogie, which gained popularity in the 1930s and became part of the big-band repertoire, such as "Boogie Woogie Bugle Boy of Company B." It formed the basis of most early rock-and-roll songs by Chuck Berry, Jerry Lee Lewis, and Elvis Presley. The R&B styles of Fats Domino and Ray Charles also came out of the 12-bar blues tradition.

The 12-bar blues is a series of chords that has 12 measures, each of which usually gets four beats. Each measure (bar) has one chord played in it. The progression can be played in a fast, medium, or slow tempo. Just three chords are used – the chords based on the I, the IV, and the V of the key. Musicians refer to these as the "one chord," the "four chord," and the "five chord." In the key of C, the I, IV, and V chords are based on C, F, and G. (The C scale is C-D-E-F-G-A-B-C.) The three chords are generally played as dominant seventh chords. In the key of C, these would be C7, F7, and G7.

The 12-bar blues is usually played in common time, i.e., 4/4 time with four beats in every bar. A chord is generally played on each beat of the bar. The 12-bar blues pattern is repeated several times. Each 12-bar section is called a "Chorus."

This book advertised that no music reading was necessary, and it isn't. Think of the example below as a map or grid. Here's a bit of explanation:

The "map" consists of five parallel, horizontal lines on which notes are written, on the lines and in the spaces. The treble clef 𝄞 at the left of the staff indicates right-hand notes. The two numbers at the beginning are called the time signature. As we noted earlier, 4/4 time means there are four beats to each bar (or measure). Each bar of four beats is separated by a bar line. Each slash indicates a chord played on one beat.

On page 16, there is an outline of the 12-bar blues pattern, with the chords represented as Roman numerals. The numerals represent chords built on notes of the scale of the key in which we are playing. We will start in the key of C. The C major scale consists of the notes C-D-E-F-G-A-B. The Roman numerals progress going upward with C as I. So I is C, IV is F, and V is G. Note that all the chords are 7th chords.

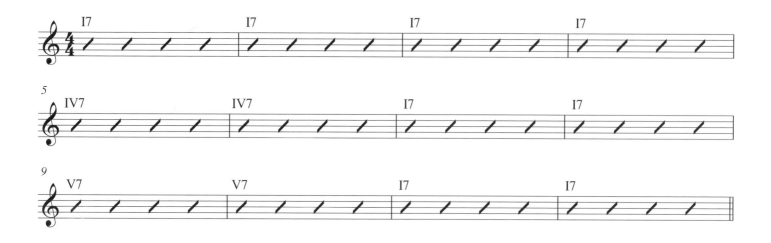

Now let's look at the same 12 bars, this time set in the key of C.

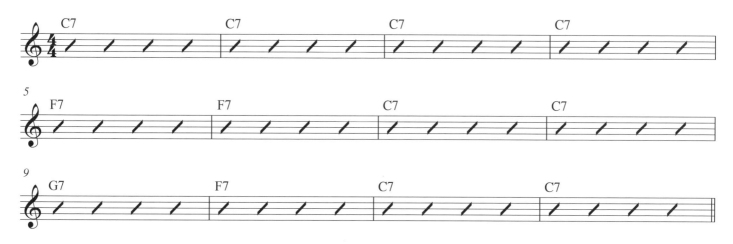

Note that there are generally four bars of I7, two bars of IV7, one bar of I7, one bar of V7, one bar of IV7, and two bars of I7. There are dozens of variations of the 12-bar blues pattern, but this is the most basic and the one we will use.

Okay, it's time to transfer this information to the keyboard. We are going to begin by playing a 12-bar blues pattern with the left hand only. The foundation of a great blues piano performance is a strong and steady left hand. However, we are not going to play full 7th chords. Let's begin by playing intervals of a 5th. It is not always necessary to play all the notes of a chord.

Here are the 5ths we are going to play to represent the chords C7, F7, and G7.

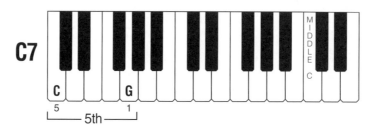

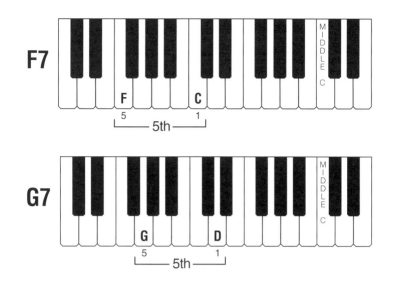

First, find these 5ths with your left hand. If you need to, refer back to the keyboard diagram on page 11 (Chapter 6). We are going to play each 5th with our left hand on each beat of the bar in a moderately slow tempo. We'll start at about 80 beats per minute (bpm). Once we get the feel for this progression, we can speed up the tempo. Here's our 12-bar blues chord pattern again. Listen to the recorded example and then try playing it.

 Track 1

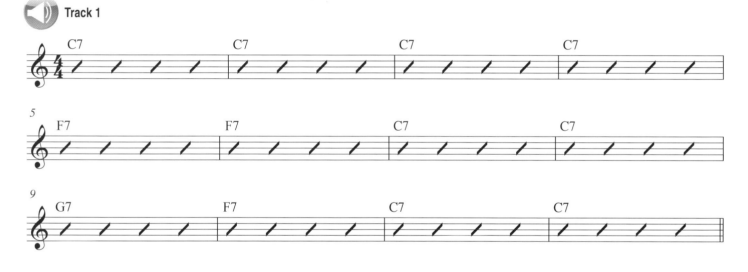

 Track 2

Next, we'll speed up the tempo a bit to the metronome mark of 100.

 Track 3

Then we'll play it at the slightly faster speed of 120 bpm.

Play the progression over and over until you have no problem playing steadily on each beat and moving from one chord position to another.

CHAPTER 9
THE BASIC LEFT-HAND PATTERN

As mentioned earlier, the foundation of a great piano blues performance is a strong and steady left-hand pattern. First learning the left-hand patterns, then adding right-hand "licks" (short melodic fragments), is the way to play blues piano. The "barrelhouse pattern" is the most established left-hand formula in blues piano.

THE BARRELHOUSE BLUES

As noted in Chapter 1, blues piano had its origins in barrelhouses in East Texas and Louisiana in the late 1800s. These were cheap drinking establishments where beer was sold from wooden barrels. Most such establishments had a battered upright piano as the center of entertainment. Pianists drifted from camp to camp looking for places to play. The pianists adapted to the limitations of the pianos with ingenuity. They developed an aggressive style to be heard above the crowd. Barrelhouse players didn't tickle the ivories – they smashed them.

The left-hand barrelhouse blues pattern consists of an alternation of the intervals of a 5th and a 6th in the left hand, played on each beat of the bar. The 5th is played on beats 1 and 3; the 6th is played on beats 2 and 4. The diagrams below show the interval of a 5th built on C and the interval of a 6th built on C.

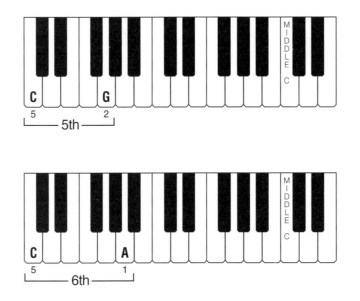

 Tracks 4–5

The keyboard diagram below shows you what notes to play in the left hand for the F7 chord. Track 4 demonstrates four bars of the pattern in C played in the left hand at 80 bpm. Track 5 consists of two bars of the pattern in F, played by the left hand at 80 bpm.

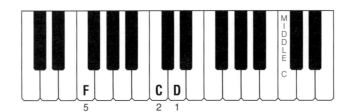

Track 6

The diagram shows what notes to play in the left hand for the G7 chord. Track 6 demonstrates one bar of the pattern in G, played by the left hand. This left-hand pattern is standard in blues piano. Pay attention to the fingering – use fingers 2 and 5 for the interval of a 5th and 1 and 5 for the interval of a 6th. That way, you don't have to move your thumb.

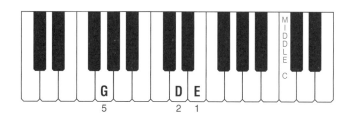

The left hand plays on each of the four beats per bar. The 5th is played on beats 1 and 3 and the 6th is played on beats 2 and 4. Here's our 12-bar blues chord progression for review:

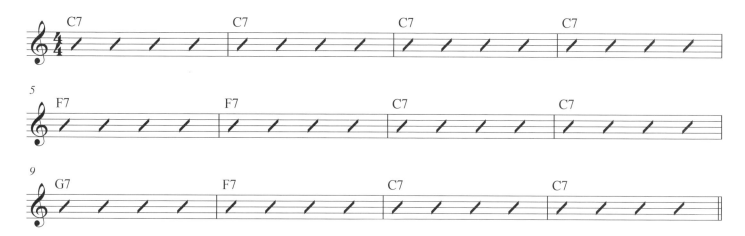

 Track 7

Listen to the recorded example and try playing the left-hand pattern for a standard 12-bar blues in C. We'll start at a fairly slow speed, 80 bpm. You'll notice that the hardest part is moving your hand from C to F and G.

 Track 8

Eventually, as you get comfortable with it, speed up to 100 bpm.

 Track 9

Practice the pattern over and over until you can play it comfortably and change chords without looking at the keys. You need to be able to play it in your sleep. Try to work up to 120 bpm.

The left-hand barrelhouse pattern can be used in almost any style of blues. When you are in doubt, or when the rhythm starts to get wobbly, it's a fall-back technique that works in almost every situation.

ADDING THE RIGHT HAND

Now we are going to play something with our right hand, with the intention of eventually putting both hands together. Keep your pinkie finger on G the whole time. We'll strike the notes each time the chord changes, and then just hold the notes.

 Track 10

Here are the tones we'll play in the right hand for each chord. For C7, play E and G simultaneously. On Track 10, the interval is played for eight beats at 80 bpm.

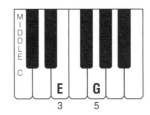

 Track 11

For F7, play E♭ and G simultaneously. On Track 11, the interval is played for eight beats at 80 bpm.

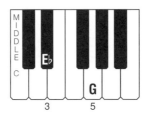

 Track 12

For G7, play D and G simultaneously. On Track 12, the interval is played for four beats.

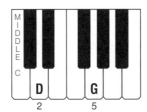

 Track 13

Listen now as the right hand plays an entire blues chorus at 80 bpm. Note that we will not be playing full chords in the right hand, just a few notes in each chord.

Okay, take a deep breath. Don't be afraid of making mistakes. This is our first real blues. Let's put the hands together throughout an entire blues chorus. We'll play the left-hand pattern we played before, along with the right-hand chord changes we just learned.

Track 14

First, listen to the example. Always play with a steady beat in the left hand. Let's start at the tempo of 80 bpm. You don't have to go fast. Playing steadily is more important. Practice this until it's solid.

 Track 15

Next, let's play the chorus a little faster, at a tempo of 100 bpm. Listen to Track 15 first, then practice until it's secure.

Track 16

Let's increase the speed a bit more, to 120 bpm. Listen to the audio track, then practice until it's solid. If you played it correctly, it should sound like a blues chorus.

Track 17

Now we'll play the same notes in the right hand, but with more rhythmic emphasis, striking the chord on beat 1 and again on the "and" of beat 2 in each bar. Listen to Track 17, then practice the right hand alone.

Track 18

Always start each new example slowly. Playing at about 80 bpm, try putting both hands together. As you get better at switching, you can speed up the tempo. Listen to Track 18.

 Track 19

First Listen to Track 19, then try playing the example at 100 bpm.

Track 20

First Listen to Track 20, then try playing the example at 120 bpm. Now we've got something that really sounds like a blues.

Track 21

Next, we'll change some notes in the right-hand figure, moving the notes up a step and then back down. Here are the notes for the C chord.

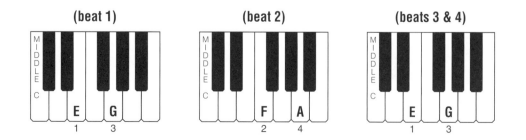

Here are the right-hand notes for the F chord.

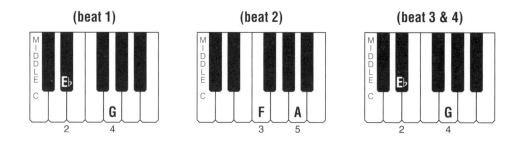

 Track 23

Here are the right-hand notes for the G chord.

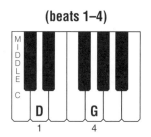

 Tracks 24–26

The left-hand figure remains the same. Listen to Track 24 at 80 bpm, then try playing it. Track 25 is 100 bpm and Track 26 is 120 bpm. Increase the tempo as you feel more and more secure.

 Tracks 27–29

Finally, we'll add some syncopation to the right hand. These are the same notes we used in Track 21 (C chord), Track 22 (F chord), and Track 23 (G chord).

 Track 30

Listen to Track 30 to hear the rhythm of the right-hand chord. Count aloud: "one, two-and."

Tracks 31–33

Track 31 includes both hands playing at about 80 bpm. Track 32 is 100 bpm and Track 33 is 120 bpm. Increase the tempo as you feel more and more secure.

CHAPTER 10

RIGHT-HAND IMPROVISATION USING THE BLUES SCALES

THE BLUES SCALES

Right-hand improvisation is one of the most characteristic elements of blues piano. To improvise in blues, we can use notes from the blues scales. There are two blues scales for each key: the major blues scale and the minor blues scale. Each blues scale contains six notes.

The C major blues scale: C-D-E♭-E-G-A-C.

The series of scale degrees starting on C: 1-2-♭3-3-5-6-1.

The half-step formula: root, up 2, up 1, up 1, up 3, up 2, up 3.

🔊 **Track 34**

Listen to the sound of the C major blues scale.

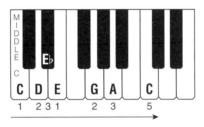

The C minor blues scale: C-E♭-F-G♭-G-B♭-C.

The series of scale degrees starting on C: 1-♭3-4-♭5-5-♭7-1.

The half-step formula: root, up 3, up 2, up 1, up 1, up 3, up 2.

🔊 **Track 35**

Listen to the sound of the C minor blues scale.

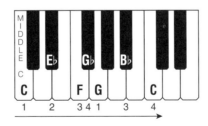

In the C minor blues scale, the pitches ♭3 (E♭), ♭5 (G♭), and ♭7 (B♭) are referred to as "blue notes." On the piano, these are an approximation because the actual pitches would be found between the piano keys. In blues singing, the vocalist typically bends these notes. Blues guitarists do the same. Notes cannot be bent on the piano, so players have developed techniques to simulate bending. We look at this in further depth in Chapter 12.

Note the different characters of these two scales. The major blues scale (Track 34) sounds fairly cheerful, while the minor blues scale (Track 35) sounds somewhat melancholy. When improvising a blues, we take notes from either blues scale and play "licks," small groups of notes (usually two to five) that make a melodic statement. A "riff" is basically a lick, but is generally a repeated phrase.

BLUES MELODIC LICKS

Blues melodic licks are usually built out of fragments of the blues scale. Let's construct some licks out of the blues scales, beginning with the C major blues scale.

 Track 36

Lick 1 is comprised of two notes.

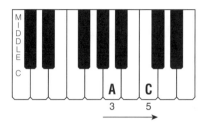

 Track 37

Lick 2 has three notes. This one works great if we can play it in triplets, i.e., with three notes on each beat. It's a little tricky, so practice it.

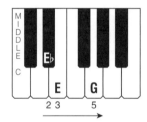

 Track 38

Here's a four-note lick, Lick 3.

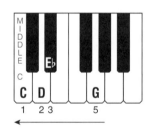

Now we have three licks based on the C major blues scale. We can easily play a whole 12-bar blues with these licks.

SWING FEEL

Before we go any further, let's discuss rhythmic "feels" in blues. Most blues are played with a "swing feel," in which the eighth notes (there are two eighth notes to every beat) are played with a lilt. The first of the two is approximately twice as long as the second. Listen to the examples on the audio tracks.

 Tracks 39–40

Track 39 is played with a straight-eighth-note feel. This is how eighth notes are generally played in classical, rock, bossa nova, and other music. Track 40 is played with a swing feel. This is how eighth notes are generally played in jazz and blues. We will play all our examples with a swing feel until we get to Chapter 13.

"Barrelhouse Blues"

Now let's use the three licks above to play an entire blues chorus: Play Lick 1 in bars 1-2, Lick 2 in bars 3-4, Lick 1 again in bars 5-6, Lick 2 again in bars 7-8, Lick 3 in bars 9-10, and Lick 2 in bars 11-12. The left-hand pattern is the same one we used for a 12-bar blues in C.

 Tracks 41–43

Listen to Track 41. It's called "Barrelhouse Blues." If you get the licks mixed up or out of order, it's not that important. Just keep playing with your right hand and keep the blues progression going with the left. Track 41 is at a tempo of about 80 bpm. Once you have the tune down, play it at a faster tempo, 100 bpm (Track 42), then even faster, at 120 bpm (Track 43).

USING THE C MINOR BLUES SCALE

Let's explore the C minor blues scale in a similar manner, using comparable licks.

 Track 44

Lick 4 employs two notes.

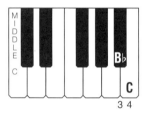

 Track 45

Lick 5 requires three notes.

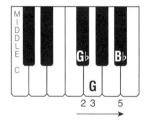

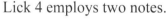 **Track 46**

Here's a four-note pattern, Lick 6.

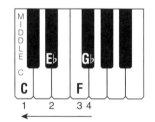

Tracks 47–49

Then we can put them together in a 12-bar blues. Play Lick 4 in bars 1-2, Lick 5 in bars 3-4, Lick 4 again in bars 5-6, Lick 5 again in bars 7-8, Lick 6 in bars 9-10, and Lick 5 in bars 11-12. The left-hand pattern is the same one we used for a 12-bar blues in C. Once you've mastered it at 80 bpm (Track 47), play it at a faster tempo, 100 bpm (Track 48), then even faster, at 120 bpm (Track 49).

So there we have it – two blues compositions. One makes use of the major blues scale and the other calls for the minor blues scale. Each has three licks. Which of the two you like better is a matter of taste. When playing a blues, you don't have to stick with one or the other. You can mix them together as much as you like.

Let's add another blues to our repertoire, this time in the key of G. We'll use the same left-hand barrelhouse pattern, but now sounding the notes G, C. and D. Study the configurations for each chord, shown in the diagrams below. Listen to the audio tracks to hear what they sound like.

Track 50

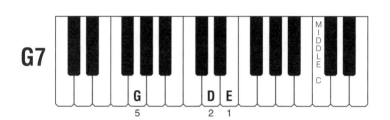

Track 51

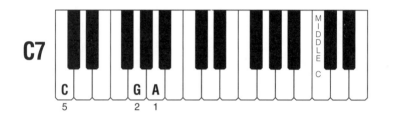

Track 52

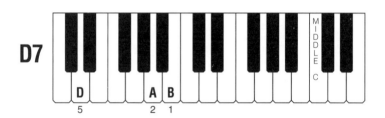

Track 53

Practice the left-hand patterns until they feel natural, then try an entire blues chorus with the left hand only. The blues pattern in the key of G is given below. The audio track is set at 100 bpm.

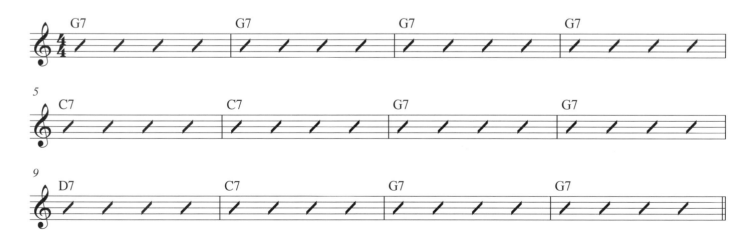

A "riff blues" is built on a single riff with slight variations. Here's Riff 1. It's in three successive intervals of 3rds as shown in the diagrams below: B-D, then C-E, then back to B-D. Listen to Track 54 to hear how the riff is played. It's repeated four times in the first four bars. Use your right hand.

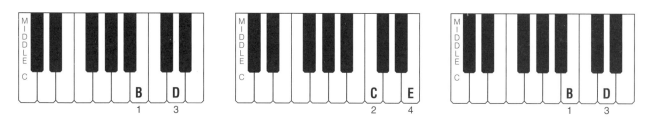

With one exception, Riff 2 is exactly the same as the first: the B♮ becomes a B♭. Play B♭-D, then C-E, then back to B♭-D

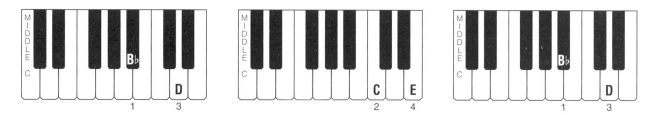

Tracks 55–57

We play Riff 1 in bars 1-4, Riff 2 in bars 5-6, Riff 1 in bars 7-9, Riff 2 in bar 10, and Riff 1 in bars 11-12. Play the right-hand part, slowly at first. Listen to Track 55 (80 bpm). Increase the tempo gradually: Track 56 (100 bpm); Track 57 (120 bpm).

Tracks 58–60

Now try both hands together at a slow tempo. We call this song "Roadhouse Blues." Listen to Track 58 (80 bpm). Increase the tempo gradually: Track 59 (100 bpm); Track 60 (120 bpm).

At this juncture, let's make up our own blues licks in the key of G, using either the G major blues scale or the G minor blues scale. The scales and their right-hand fingerings are given below.

Track 61

Here's the G major blues scale:

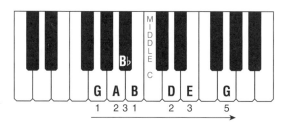

Track 62

Here's the G minor blues scale:

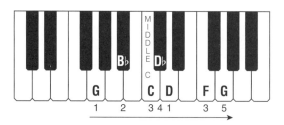

Take a look at these ideas for creating right-hand licks and improvising:

Track 63

Licks can ascend.

Track 64

Licks can descend.

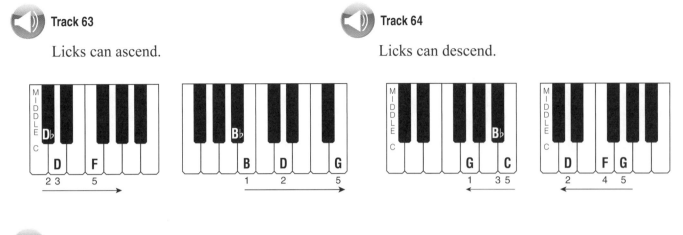

Track 65

Licks can go both ways.

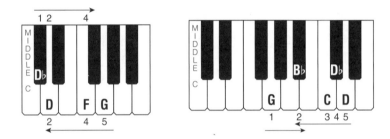

Track 66

Blues is full of repetitions. Sometimes you can play a short lick and repeat the exact same lick many times, or you can vary a lick by changing the rhythms and not the notes.

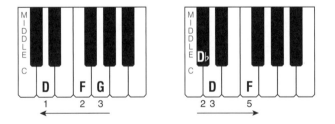

Track 67

If you're not familiar with improvisation, don't panic! It's not a big deal. Here, one of our play-along tracks (Track 197) can be used. Listen to "Roadhouse Blues" (Track 67). This blues chorus works quite well for adding licks from Tracks 63, 64, and 65 – or your own licks.

CHAPTER 12
SPECIAL BLUES TECHNIQUES

GRACE NOTES

Grace notes are one of several special techniques used in blues piano. In blues, grace notes are often referred to as "crushed" notes or "bent" notes.

Whereas human voices, stringed instruments, and wind instruments can bend a tone by sliding it sharp or flat, the piano is made up of 88 discrete notes. Thus, we use grace notes to imitate bent notes. We usually slide into the note from the one right below. Grace notes can make a melody more interesting.

 Track 68

Unlike classical technique, when playing the blues, the same finger is often used on a single stroked grace note to slide into the melody tone

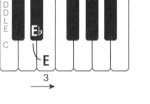

 Track 69

Most frequently, grace notes are applied either by half step or whole step from below the melody note. However, it is possible to apply a grace note from above the melody note.

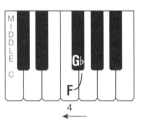

 Track 70

We can also use double or triple grace notes, when playing an interval such as a 3rd.

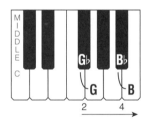

 Track 71

If we added a grace note to the first lick we learned in Chapter 10 (page 24), it would look and sound like this.

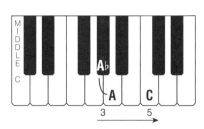

TREMOLO

A tremolo is a rapid oscillation between two distinct notes or combinations of notes. On the keyboard, a quick rocking motion between the fingers of one hand produces the tremolo. Tremolos can consist of an octave, of smaller intervals (3rds and 6ths are common), or of full chords.

Track 72

To play a tremolo, choose an interval larger than a whole step (such as a 3rd, shown below) and alternate playing the two notes as quickly as possible. Your fingers are "rolling" between the two notes. In fact, a tremolo is sometimes called a roll. Play this one in your right hand.

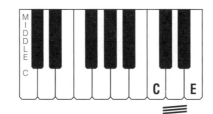

Track 73

As noted above, tremolos frequently occur on 3rds, 6ths, or octaves. Again, try these in your right hand.

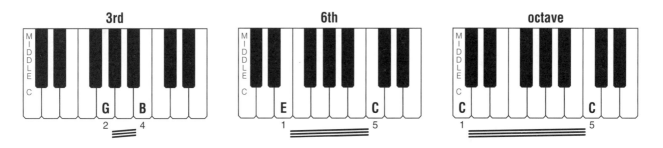

Track 74

Sometimes a tremolo consists of a whole chord; try rolling an F chord in your right hand. Tremolos can even be performed with two hands at once; have a go at the C7 chord.

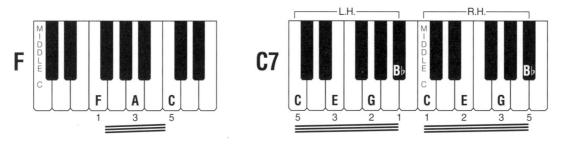

Track 75

Tremolos can be combined with other ornamentations. Here is a classic figure – a tremolo between the 3rd and 5th of a major chord, embellished with a grace note (E♭, in this case).

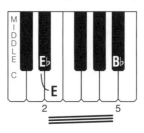

Track 76

Tremolo technique features prominently in this short blues solo. The left hand plays a typical barrelhouse pattern. The piece itself is based on a single riff with variations. The notes of the right-hand riff are shown below: G-B♭, then F-A, then E-G.

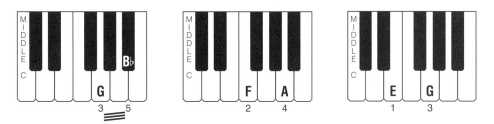

This riff is played in bars 1-2 and 3-4. Then the same riff is played in bars 5-6, except that the E♮ becomes E♭. The original riff appears in bars 7-8 and 11-12.

Track 77

In bar 9 the notes B-D are played, as shown in the diagram below.

Track 78

The notes A-C are played in bar 10.

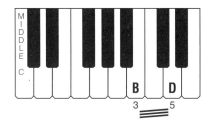

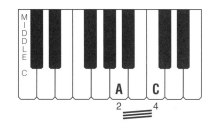

Track 79

Listen to the audio track, which is the right hand only, then try it yourself. Just the right hand. Then, put both hands to work by adding our typical left-hand barrelhouse bass figuration.

Track 80

This tune is called "Back at the Turkey Shack." Give it a listen.

MELODIC LEAD-INS

Blues often have melodic lead-ins, short phrases that lead to a target note. Listen to the two right-hand examples that follow, then play them on the piano using the diagrams.

Track 81

Track 82

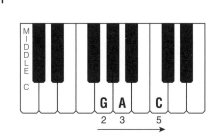

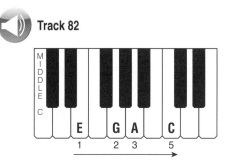

We could base a whole 12-bar chorus on the melodic lead-in shown here (Track 83). Play this right-hand riff 12 times over the barrelhouse pattern in C. (Track 84 is set at 110 bpm.)

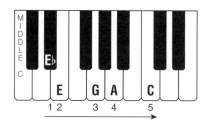

DOUBLING THE RHYTHM OF THE LEFT HAND

Track 85

We're going to get our left hand working harder by playing two eighth notes on each beat rather than a single quarter note. Doing the math, we realize that there are eight eighth notes in a measure of 4/4 time. This is where the term "eight to the bar" comes from. We'll play the two eighth notes of each beat in a swing feel (long-short). Let's practice the left hand for a blues in C using eighth notes. Start slowly, about 80 bpm. Listen to Track 85.

Track 86

Now that we've got that down, let's add a right-hand part. We'll use six riffs. Riff 1 features parallel 3rds and is used leading into bars 1, 5, and 11.

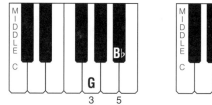 

Track 87

Riff 2 is repeated 3rds in eighth notes, and is used in bars 2 and 6.

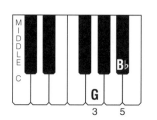

Track 88

Riff 3 is 3rds in a syncopated rhythm, and is used in bars 3 and 7.

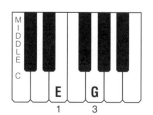

Track 89

Riff 4 is the same as Riff 1 except that the E♮ becomes an E♭.

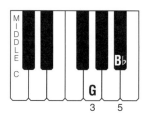 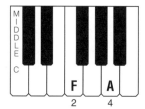 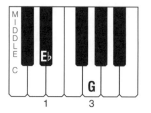

Riff 5 is simply held notes used in bars 9 and 10.

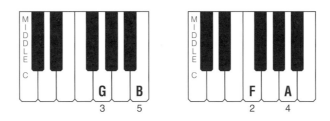

 Track 91

Riff 6 is a repeated three-note pattern used in bar 12.

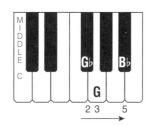

 Track 92

Practice each of the riffs separately, then try the 12-bar chorus with the right hand only (80 bpm). When you feel confident that you can manage it with both hands, listen to Track 92.

CHAPTER 13

STRAIGHT-EIGHTH-NOTE BLUES

So far, we have been playing everything with swing-eighth notes. But blues sometimes uses straight-eighth notes. The groove has a different feel.

Marcia Ball (born 1949) is a blues singer/pianist who grew up in Louisiana, but who's lived most of her life in Austin, Texas. Her blues style is a mixture of New Orleans influences and Texas blues. She has cited Professor Longhair as a role model, so it's not surprising that one of her most popular songs is her rendition of Professor Longhair's "Red Beans." The next piece is in the style of Marcia Ball's "Red Beans."

Here, we are going to double the rhythm of the left hand so that two eighth notes are played on each beat, as we did in the last piece. However, we're going to play it in straight eighths, in the key of G. First we must learn to play the left hand through the entire form in that key, using eighth notes in a straight rhythm

 Track 93

Here are the notes we use in the left hand, built upon G (I), C (IV), and D (V) in the key of G.

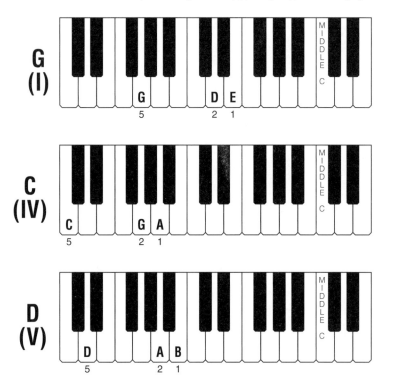

Practice the left-hand part. Begin slowly, about 110 bpm, then gradually increase the tempo. Ultimately we want to do this song at a pretty quick pace, about 140 bpm.

Track 94

Next, note the following four right-hand licks. Lick 1 uses the major blues scale. We use grace notes sliding into the B.

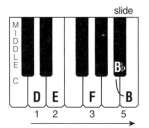

Track 95

Lick 2 is the scale going up and coming down.

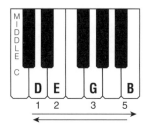

Track 96

Lick 3 is the same lick as Lick 1,
except the B♮ is changed to B♭.

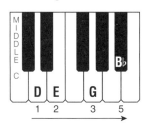

Track 97

Lick 4 is exactly like Lick 2,
except the B♮ is replaced by B♭.

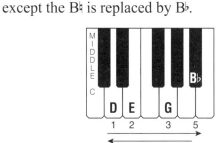

Track 98

Then we play Lick 1 and Lick 4 again.

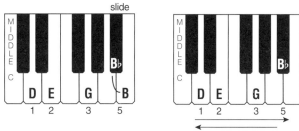

Track 99

Try the piece with both hands.

Track 100

We can add a second chorus and add four more new licks. Over the G7 chord, we can alternate two new licks. The first is basically Lick 1 backward.

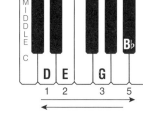

Track 101

Our new Lick 2 is simply a grace note sliding from B♭ to B♮, played four times.

New Lick 3 is essentially old Lick 3 backward.

Finally, new Lick 4 is simply the B♭ repeated four times.

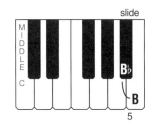

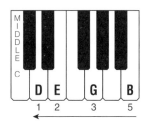

Track 102

Play new Lick 1 in bars 1, 3, 7, 9, and 11. Play new Lick 2 (Track 101) in bars 2, 4, 8, and 12. Play new Lick 3 in bar 5. Play new Lick 4 in bars 6 and 10. Listen to the entire second chorus as played on Track 102, then try it for yourself.

Jerry Lee Lewis (born 1935) is a terrific example of a boogie-woogie and blues pianist. One of the pioneers of rock-and-roll, his hit songs include "Great Balls of Fire" and "Whole Lotta Shakin' Goin On." Most of the early rock-and-roll songs were based on a 12-bar blues progression, and the final example in Chapter 13 is close to Lewis's early rock-and-roll style. He often performed a barrelhouse (or similar) pattern in his left hand. Lewis generally made use of the major blues scale, rather than the minor blues scale.

Jerry Lee preferred straight eighths, a typical feature of rock-and-roll, as opposed to the swing music that preceded it. He also used repeated notes, repeated chords, repeated intervals, and repeated octaves. (Repetition is a characteristic of blues in general.)

 Track 103

Here's an example of repeated notes in eighth notes. (With the exception of Track 110, all the examples in this chapter are played with the right hand.)

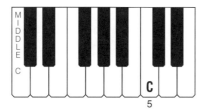

 Track 104

Repeated intervals of a 3rd have a great blues sound.

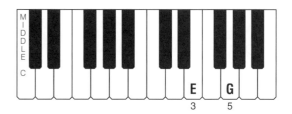

 Track 105

Repeated octaves have a nice ringing sound on the piano.

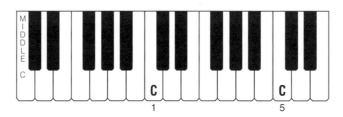

REPEATED CHORDS

 Track 106

Lewis's right hand was characterized by repeated chords (usually V7 chords) banged out in a propulsive eighth-note rhythm. He sometimes played a ♭3rd in the repeated I7 chords, giving the music a raucous quality. Don't hesitate to use repeated notes, intervals or chords.

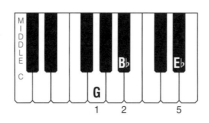

GLISSANDO

Lewis was best known for his use of *glissando*, a slide or glide on the piano keys. (He practically made a career out of it!) The pseudo-Italian term comes from the French word glisser, "to slide," and is abbreviated as *gliss*. It can either ascend or descend; descending glissandos are more common. Glissandos can use either the white keys or the black keys; white key glissandos are more common.

🔊 **Track 107**

To perform an ascending glissando, place the nail of your right middle finger on a low white note with the nail facing right. Drag your finger up from left to right across the keys toward the top of the keyboard. When you perform a glissando, make sure that only your fingernails touch the keys, because it's easy to break your cuticle if you drag skin across the keys.

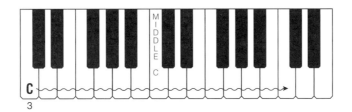

🔊 **Track 108**

To perform a descending glissando, place the thumbnail of your right hand on a high white note with your thumbnail facing left. Drag your thumb down from right to left across the keys toward the lower keys

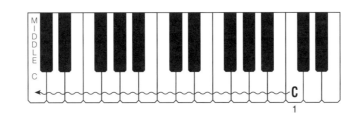

🔊 **Track 109**

Lewis used both ascending and descending glissandos, glisses with both hands going different ways, etc. – almost compulsively.

PUTTING IT ALL TOGETHER

Track 110

The music example for Lewis-style rock-and-roll begins with the left-hand barrelhouse pattern played in double time, at 140 bpm

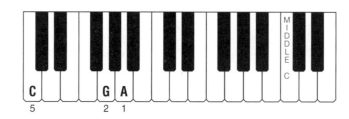

Track 111

In the right hand, there is a four-note figure used repeatedly in bars 1-4.

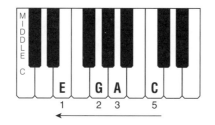

Track 112

A four-note riff works well over the F7 chord in bars 5-6.

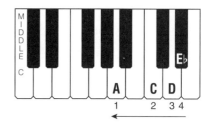

Track 113

Repeated chords are effective in bars 9 and 10.

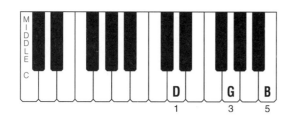 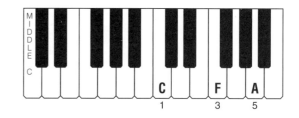

Track 114

Make use of a glissando in bar 12.

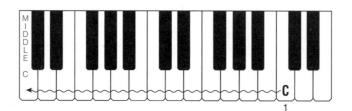

Track 115

Listen to Track 115 to hear a full performance of the first chorus.

Track 116

A second chorus can include other rock-and-roll techniques – for instance, a repeated E♭ chord in bars 1-4. The ♭3rd in the chord seems dissonant and strident in the C major tonality.

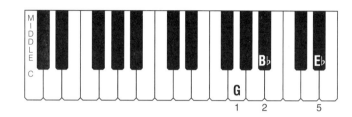

For bar 4, throw in an ascending glissando.

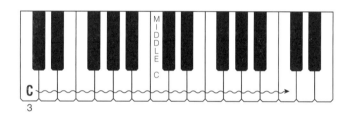

Track 117

A three-note figure, played as fast as possible, works well in bars 11-12

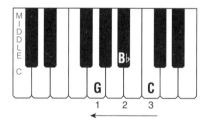

Track 118

Let's put a whole chorus together. Listen to Track 118.

CHAPTER 15

GOSPEL BLUES

The musical genres of gospel, jazz, blues, and boogie-woogie all arose at about the same time and from the same sources. The time period was approximately the 1880s through the 1920s, and the place was East Texas and Louisiana. The styles were the result of interaction between blacks of African descent, with their African music influences, and white Americans, with their European musical influences.

In southern ports like New Orleans, considered to be the birthplace of jazz, there were also Caribbean musical influences. Jelly Roll Morton referred to these as "The Spanish Tinge."

Black gospel music grew out of the spirituals created by African slaves, who fused African music and religion with the traditional Christianity and hymns of the slave-owners. Spirituals are ubiquitous in our society – nearly everyone is familiar with tunes like "He's Got the Whole World in His Hands," "Kum Ba Yah," "This Little Light of Mine," and "Deep River."

Because of their similar roots, there's a lot of crossover in the genres of gospel and blues. Some even claim that you can turn any blues tune into a gospel tune by substituting the word "God" for the word "baby," or make any gospel tune into a blues tune by doing the opposite.

 Track 119

"When the Saints Go Marching In" is a spiritual that's also become a jazz and blues standard. When played by a Dixieland jazz band, it's usually cast as a bright swing tune with a walking bass. Listen to the recorded example, played at 170 bpm.

 Track 120

It's also commonly played in a "stride" style. Track 120 is played at 124 bpm.

 Track 121

It can also be treated in a fast "romp" style, using our barrelhouse left-hand pattern. You can play the right-hand melody using a five-finger position with the thumb starting on middle C. The hand doesn't have to move. Here are the first few notes of the melody.

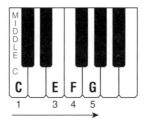

The chords are the same three used in a 12-bar blues, but this example is a 16-bar tune and the chords come in a slightly different order. The chord progression is shown below. For an example of a one-chorus performance, listen to Track 122.

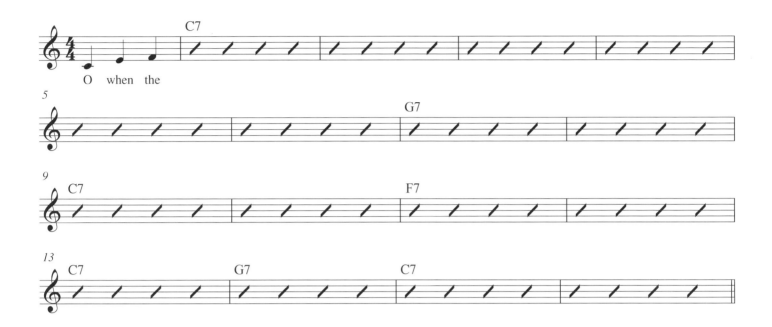

Boogie woogie is a jazz style based on the 12-bar blues progression. It rose to prominence in the 1930s. "Eight to the bar" – playing eight eighth notes in the left hand in each measure – is how this style is often described. The repetitious boogie patterns used in the left hand are its most identifying characteristic and usually outline the basic chord progression.

Track 123

There are many common boogie-woogie patterns. Several are demonstrated on Track 123 at 150 bpm.

Track 124

The boogie-woogie figure we are going to use is based on exactly the same notes used in the left hand for the barrelhouse pattern. In the boogie-woogie style, the notes are played individually, instead of two at once. Here are the patterns in the key of C are shown below. Listen to the pattern on Track 124, then practice it on the keyboard, starting slowly at first. The recording is at 150 bpm.

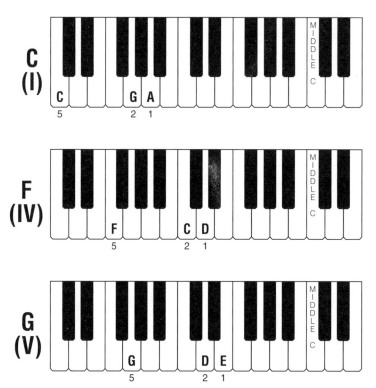

Track 125

In the first chorus of our boogie-woogie example, there are four right-hand riffs. Riff 1, based on parallel descending 3rds, is played in bars 1, 2, 3, 4, 7, 8, 11, and 12.

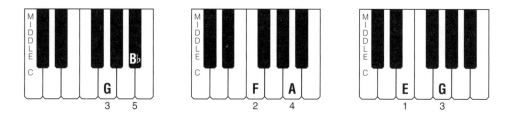

Track 126

Riff 2, is the same pattern, only a 4th higher. It's played in bars 6 and 7.

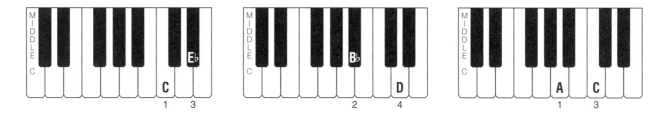

 Track 127

Bars 9 and 10 simply have held 3rds.

 Track 128

Play both hands. Ultimately, the pattern should be performed at about 150 bpm, as on the recording, but it is a good idea to practice it slowly and build up the speed.

Track 129

The second chorus is based on a lead-in pattern. The pattern is played in bars 1, 2, 3, 4, 7, 8, 11, and 12.

Track 130

The same pattern, a 4th higher is played in bars 5 and 6.

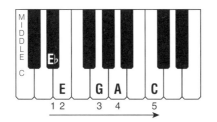

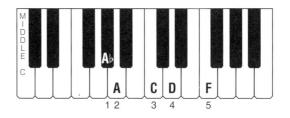

Track 131

Bars 9 and 10 have the same held 3rds as in Track 127. Now listen to Track 131 and play the entire second chorus.

Boogie woogie can be performed at a moderate tempo or brightly. Ultimately, the goal is to play it as quickly and accurately as possible. Boogie woogie is often played at tempos that aren't even on the standard metronome.

SLOW BLUES IN 12/8

A slow blues is typically played in 12/8 meter. The 12/8 meter has 12 eighth notes per bar, with each bar being divided into four strong pulses with three eighth notes falling on each pulse.

Tracks 132–134

To get the sound of a slow blues in your ear, listen to Track 132. The right hand generally plays repeated V7 chords on each of the 12 eighth notes. The left hand can play a root note at the beginning of each bar (Track 133) or on each strong pulse (Track 134). These patterns are basically accompaniment patterns for a singer or soloist.

Track 135

Our slow 12/8 blues is in G major. The chords we'll use in the right hand are G7 (I7), C7 (IV7), and D7 (V7). Here they are:

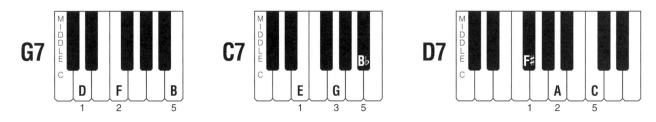

Track 136

Try the right-hand pattern for an entire chorus.

Track 137

Then add the left hand, simply playing the root of the chord at the beginning of each bar, for an entire chorus.

Track 138

In 12/8 slow blues, you can play eighth-note arpeggios (broken chords) with the right hand. Then you can add bass notes at the beginning of each bar in the left hand. An arpeggio for G7 can be played as G-B-D-F-D-B-G. Each arpeggio spans an interval of a minor 7th, with the notes going up and then coming down. Listen to Track 138, played at 60 bpm.

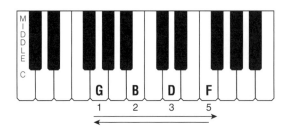

Even though the slow blues has a relaxed pulse, the right hand can play very fast licks, using notes from either of the G blues scales. These licks are usually performed with four or five fingers within the span of the interval of a 5th. Below are some examples. All are six-note riffs.

Track 139

Track 140

Track 141

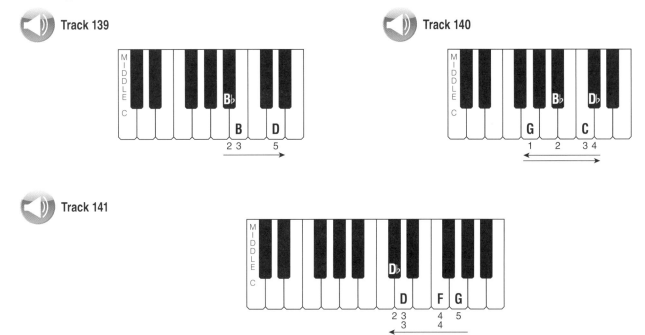

FUNKY BLUES

Many blues artists have recorded blues with a funky feel. Funk emphasizes the rhythmic groove of the interlocking parts played by the electric guitar, bass, drums, and keyboard. The groove in funk is almost always a straight-eighth groove.

Ever wonder what that down-and-dirty flavor is in funky blues? It's a chord called an augmented 9th. Its essential members are the major 3rd, the ♭7th, and the ♭3rd. Let's start with this funky voicing for the C7 chord.

The chord is usually stacked this way, from the lowest to the highest notes: the major 3rd, the ♭7th, and the ♭3rd. The root is sounded either by the bass player or by the pianist's left hand. The following diagrams show the funky three-note voicings for C7♯9, F7♯9, and G7♯9 in the right hand.

Track 142

Track 143

Track 144

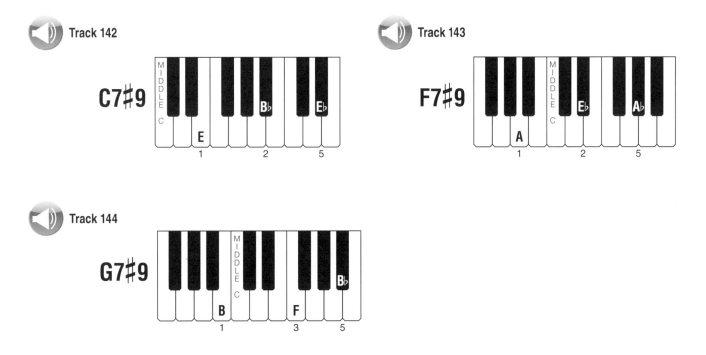

Track 145

We are going to do a funky blues inspired by James Brown. Here, the left hand doesn't play, as the electric bass has the most prominent part. The right hand plays the funky voiced chords in a syncopated pattern as in Track 145 (116 bpm).

Track 146

Here's our funky blues example. The right hand could play licks that we've learned so far in the key of C, or make up licks using either the C major blues scale or the C minor blues scale. Be aware that this tune uses straight-eighth notes and that many of our licks so far have used swing-eighth notes.

MINOR BLUES STYLE

Blues are sometimes in minor keys. In most minor blues, the I and IV chords are played as minor 7th chords and the V chord is played as a V7. In our example of a minor blues, we are going to keep it simple and play triads in the left hand, rather than 7th chords.

Track 147

We will play in the key of C minor. Our chords are Cm (i), Fm (iv), and G (V). The diagrams show how they are played with the left hand. The chords are sounded as whole notes on the first beat of every bar.

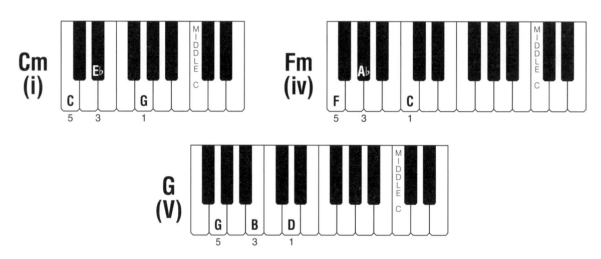

The chord pattern is a standard 12-bar blues with minor chords substituting for 7th chords.

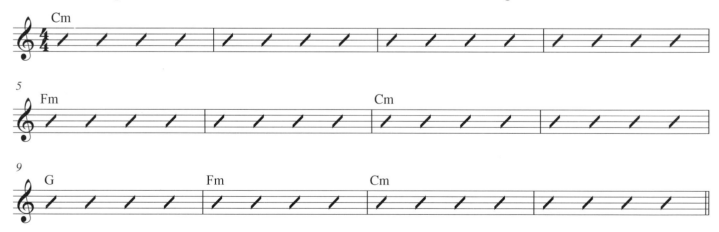

Track 148

Play the left hand by itself. Each chord is played on beat 1 and beat 2+, giving the music a syncopated feel.

Tracks 149—150

The right-hand melody is simple. There are two licks, which are played in succession three times in the 12-bar chorus (Track 149). Play the right hand by itself, then add the left hand and play them together.

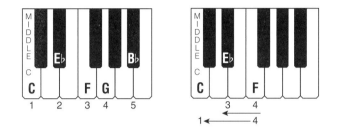

NEW ORLEANS RHUMBA BOOGIE

Blues pianist and singer Professor Longhair (Henry Roeland Byrd, 1918-1980) was known as The Godfather of New Orleans Piano. Affectionately referred to as Fess, every New Orleans pianist after him has acknowledged his influence, especially Dr. John.

Track 151

Fess made a significant contribution to the blues genre by taking a syncopated bass line and turning it into a beat commonly called the "Rhumba Boogie." This beat blended Afro-Cuban and Caribbean influences with the blues. It is played in straight eighths at a moderately slow tempo. Our track is in G. The left-hand bass line has three notes, outlining a triad.

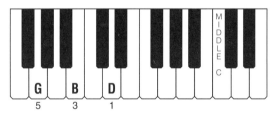

Track 152

This bass line can be spiced up with a grace note sliding into the second note of the pattern.

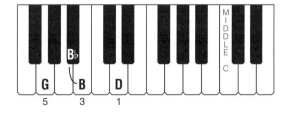

Following are some right-hand licks Professor Longhair might play over the Rhumba Boogie beat. It's difficult to play the left hand when playing a right-hand solo, so the pianist can drop the left hand during the right-hand solo.

Track 153

This lick can be played in bars 1, 2, 3, 4, 7, and 8.

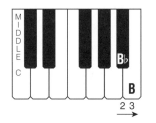

Track 154

This lick can be played in bars 2, 4, and 8.

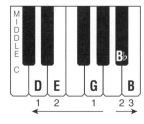

Track 155

This lick can be played in bars 5 and 6.

Track 156

This lick can be played in bar 6.

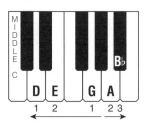

Track 157

This dyad (two-note chord) can be played in bar 9.

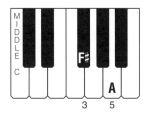

Track 158

This dyad can be played in bar 10.

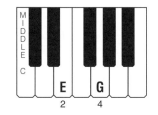

Track 159

This lick can be repeated in bars 11 and 12. It can be varied rhythmically, from playing it in a moderate speed to as fast as possible.

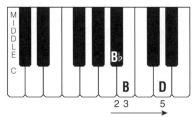

Track 160

Finally, here's the whole track.

CHAPTER 18

USING TRITONES

The tritone is an interval equal to the sum of three whole steps, thus its name. When playing the blues, it can be used effectively in place of a complete V7 chord. The tritone works well in the left hand when performing with a bass player. The bass will lay down the roots of the chords; the addition of the tritone creates a chord that sounds nice and complete.

Track 161

In blues, tritones are comprised of the 3rd and the 7th of the chords. The tritones can be played with either the 3rd or the 7th on the bottom. For example, if playing a blues in C, you could use the following tritones for the three chords – C7, F7, and G7 in the left hand.

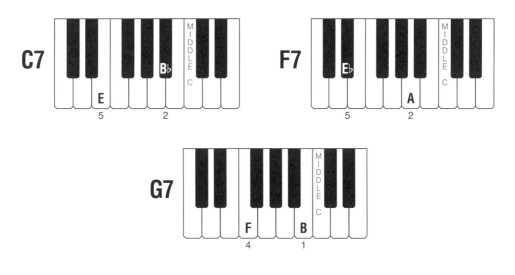

Track 162

In the previous example, the first tritone has the 3rd on the bottom and the next two have the 7th on the bottom. However, you could also play the chords in the following manner:

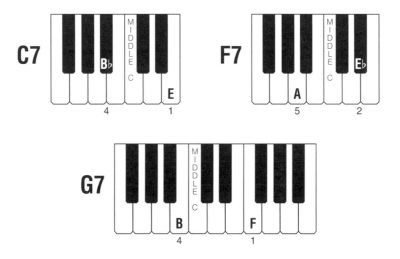

In the example above, the C7 has the 7th on the bottom and the other two chords have the 3rd on the bottom. The idea is to use tritones that are close to each other on the keyboard, so that your hand movement is minimized.

Track 163

The following blues in G employs tritones in the left hand. Here are the tritones we will use:

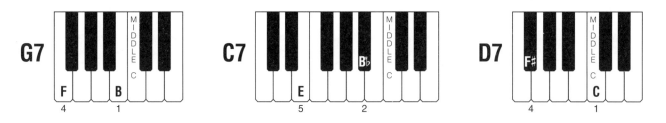

 Track 164

We've given the tritones a characteristic rhythm, hitting on beat 1 and the "and" of beat 2 in each bar. This sort of left-hand pattern works well only when playing with a bassist. Listen to the left hand by itself and then try it.

 Track 165

The right hand is built upon a single lead-in type riff in two parts. This riff is repeated six times. Listen to Track 165 and then try the right hand by itself.

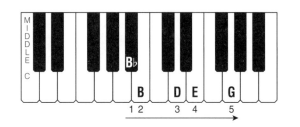 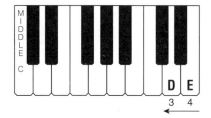

 Track 166

Once you feel comfortable playing hands separately, try putting both hands together.

 Track 167

For a second chorus, let's use a lick with parallel 3rds. Listen to the audio track, then try playing it. Observe how the notes are used rhythmically.

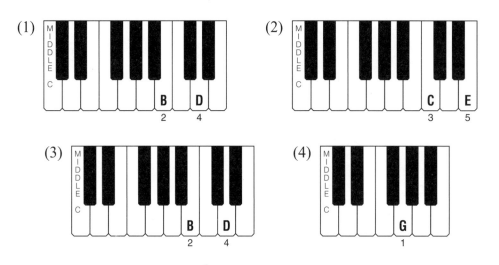

Note that in bars 5, 6, and 10, the lick is the same except that the B♮ becomes a B♭.

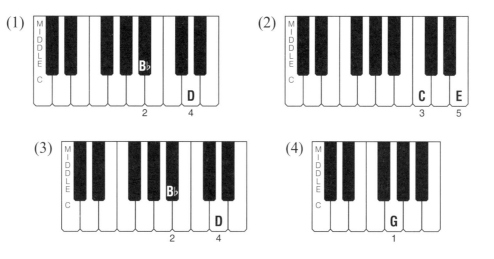

Track 169

The riff in Track 167 is used in every bar except 5, 6, and 10. In those measures, the riff in Track 168 is used.

The use of tritones sounds a little jazzier and a little more "hip" than the classic barrelhouse pattern. This style is often found in the relaxed, laid-back West Coast style of blues typified by Charles Brown.

JUMP BLUES

In Chapter 10, we looked at various blues styles. Let's add another genre to our bag of tricks. The jump blues is a style that features up-tempo, happy, often humorous songs with a danceable shuffle rhythm. The greatest proponent of jump blues was bandleader Louis ("Louie") Jordan (1908-1975) and his band, the Tympany Five. The band had dozens of hits in the 1940s and 1950s. Jordan, who was a singer and sax player, wrote and recorded humorous songs such as "Caldonia (What Makes Your Big Head So Hard?)," "Choo Choo Ch'Boogie," "There Ain't Nobody Here But Us Chickens," and "Is You Is or Is You Ain't (Ma Baby)." These songs have become blues standards.

Track 170

Jump blues songs often make use of repeated instrumental riffs. These may be repeated exactly, or the notes can be altered slightly to fit the chords, as in the following example. Tritones work well in jump blues songs, so let's build the left-hand part on the tritones we used before in the key of G.

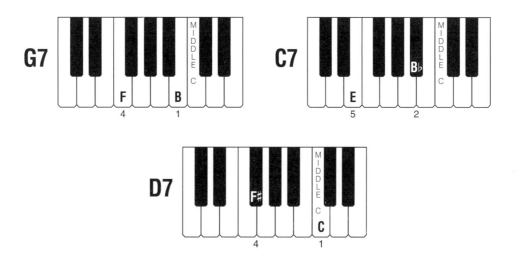

Track 171

The right hand in our jump blues is built on one riff divided into two parts:

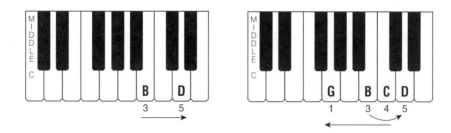

Track 172

At bars 5-6 and 9-10, the B♮s become B♭s. Otherwise the riff is repeated verbatim six times. Play the right hand by itself.

Track 173

Then put both hands together.

Track 174

A second chorus is based on a bebop-like lick.

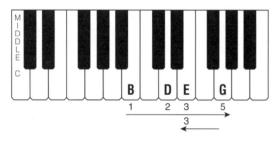

This lick is played in bars 1-4, then played exactly the same in bars 5-6, except that the B♮s become B♭s.

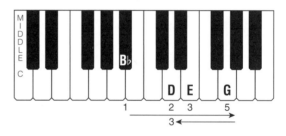

The initial lick is played again in bars 7-8. It's also played in bars 11-12. Bars 9-10 have the following lick, repeated as fast as possible. Listen to Track 175, then try playing the entire chorus.

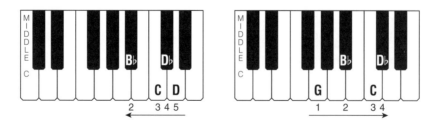

Track 175

Listen to Track 175, then try playing the entire chorus.

CHAPTER 19

BLUES INTROS & ENDINGS

INTROS FOR FAST BLUES

 Track 176

There are many ways to begin a quick 12-bar blues. A conventional one is to play the last four bars of the 12-bar blues progression and add a V7 chord in the last bar. For example, refer back to Track 1 on page 17. Here are the right-hand configurations you might use in bars 9-12:

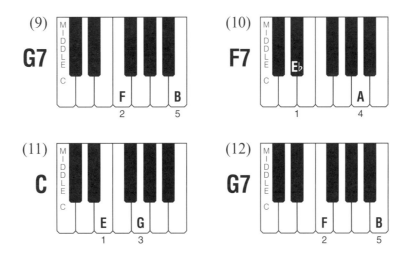

Track 177

The chord progression I7-IV7-I7 – with a lead into the V7 chord – forms another frequently played intro. This variety often has a melodic lead-in to the first chord (i.e., the first four melodic notes in this example).

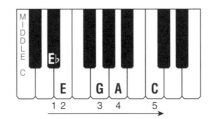

Track 178

If you're playing a blues with a standard bass pattern, such as the barrelhouse pattern or any of the boogie-woogie style left-hand patterns, you can begin simply by playing the left-hand pattern for a few bars. It's a "vamp till ready" situation. After vamping for a while (say, four bars), everyone can join in; that becomes bar 1 of the 12-bar blues progression. Here's a familiar pattern, the boogie left hand in C:

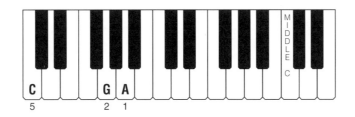

The right hand can play a lick like the one below (Track 179). Then, the two hands together sound like Track 180. Learn various blues intros. All of them are useful – and you never know what will be expected of you at a blues gig.

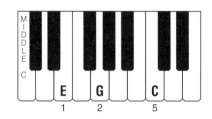

INTROS FOR SLOW BLUES

 Track 181

For a typical intro to a 12/8 slow blues (see page 44), play the last four bars of the blues progression, with a V7 chord in the last bar. Listen to the recorded example. You'll hear repeated triplet triads in the right hand. The chords, in the key of G, are D7, C7, G7, and D7. The left hand a plays a bass note at each chord change.

 Track 182

An intro to a slow blues can sometimes be as simple as an arpeggiated V7 chord, using both hands. The notes of the chord should be played from the bottom to the top, as in this G7 chord example:

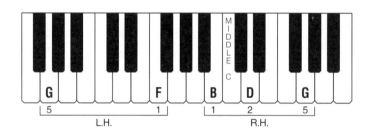

 Track 183

Here, we have a G7#5 chord, using both hands. This is a 7th chord in which the third note from the bottom (D#) is one half step higher than normal.

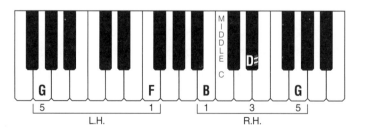

BLUES ENDINGS

Track 184

Blues endings occur over bars 11 and 12 of the 12-bar form. The I7 chord is usually played in bars 11 and 12. But blues generally end with a V7-I progression. A typical blues ending might include a bass walk-up that goes from I7 to V7 back up to I7. Note that your left hand crosses over itself to play all these notes.

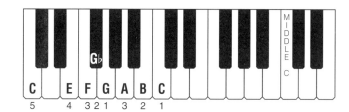

Track 185

For a common alternative, use a right-hand walk-down from I7 to V7 to I7. Here again, you have to cross your hand over.

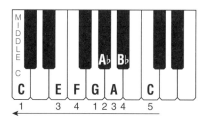

Track 186

These two ideas are often combined by putting the descending line in the right hand and the ascending line in the left. This results in a classic blues ending, as demonstrated on Track 186.

CHAPTER 20

ONCE MORE, WITH FEELING

Playing music isn't just about playing the right notes at the right time. It's also about playing them in the right way.

DYNAMICS

Dynamics are volume levels, or gradations of loudness and softness in the flow of music. How loudly or softly you play at different times can make an enormous difference to the character of the music. For instance, a haunting ballad might be played initially at a soft level, while a dramatic moment in the music might be played loudly.

Dynamic changes can be abrupt – suddenly going from soft to loud or loud to soft for dramatic purposes. Or dynamic changes can be gradual – becoming increasingly louder to build excitement or, perhaps, slowly dying out.

TEMPO

Tempo is the rate of speed at which a song is performed. As we've noted, tempo is measured in beats per minute (bpm), using a metronome. Ballads in 12/8 are usually performed slowly. Tunes with a swing feel can be performed at a medium tempo or brisk tempo (100 to 150 bpm). Boogie woogie can be performed at break-neck tempos –150 bpm or more. Oscar Peterson played some boogie woogie at 250 bpm, which isn't even on the standard metronome.

In sheet music, tempos are indicated by general words such as "Brightly" or "Moderately" or by a metronome mark (or both), giving the number of beats per minute, such as ♩ = 96.

Many songs, especially popular standards, lend themselves to various tempos. For example, "Autumn Leaves" can be performed very slowly as a melancholy ballad, at a medium tempo, or as a fast swing number. Sometimes you can put a new spin on a song by performing it at an unusual tempo.

EXPRESSION

On the piano, one can play notes smoothly or detached. Playing smoothly (*legato*) works well on ballads. Playing detached (*staccato*) can add rhythmic thrust to a blues rock number or a swing blues at a brisk tempo.

Always consider using contrasts in dynamics, tempo, and expression to add flair to your playing.

CHAPTER 21
PLAYING IN A BLUES BAND

Backing up a singer or soloist in a blues combo is known by musicians as "comping," which is short for "accompanying." Comping involves chordal playing and occasionally adding fills between vocal or melodic phrases. Rather than solo improvisation, what's important in comping is to keep the rhythm and harmony going and to complement and support the soloist, not to compete with him.

Often, in a combo situation, keyboard comping chords are played with both hands in rhythmic patterns that are accented and syncopated. The bass player in the combo will handle all the bass lines. Track 187 demonstrates a comping pattern – known as the "Charleston" rhythm – for the first four bars of a blues in C. The chords are spread between the hands.

Track 187

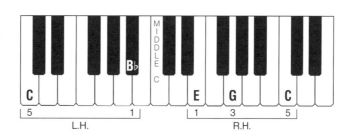

Track 188

Here's comping rhythm for two bars that use our familiar boogie-woogie pattern in the left hand. The right hand plays the same pattern as in the previous example.

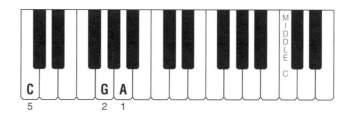

Track 189

You should also know the typical comping pattern for a slow blues in 12/8. (See page 44.) The right-hand notes are shown below. The left hand can play the root of the chord at the beginning of each bar.

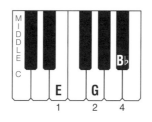

Track 190

Oftentimes, when playing in a combo, you will continue to use the barrelhouse left-hand pattern, while articulating chords in the right hand in an accented, rhythmic style. Track 190 employs the same right-hand chord as Track 187.

Track 191

You can also double the rhythm of the left hand and play eighth notes, instead of quarter notes, as demonstrated on Track 191.

CHAPTER 22
IMPROVISATION IDEAS

Here, we offer some general ideas for sparking your creativity and blues improvisations. Take any you find helpful and forget the rest.

- **Question and Answer.** Ask a question in one phrase and answer it in the next.

- **Steps and leaps.** Use both steps and leaps in your right hand.

- **Use repeated notes.** You don't have to follow a note with a different note. Sometimes the same note will do. Repetition is one of the most fundamental characteristics of the blues.

 Track 192

- **Leave space** (rests) in your music. You need not fill up each space with notes. It's better to have too little happening than too much.

Track 193

- **Play in different registers of the piano.** This is an effective way to change the tone color and the texture. Track 193 is the last four bars of a blues in C. Notice how much of the range of the piano it covers from high to low. By the way, that run down is simply the C minor blues scale. The fingering is shown here.

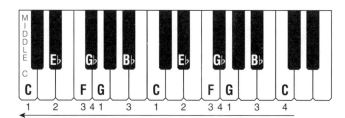

Track 194

- **Use just a few notes** and do a lot with them, instead of doing little with lots of notes. A good player can make an entire solo out of a couple of notes. Track 194 uses just two melodic notes: G and F.

- **Learn from the masters.** It is a mistake to think you must reinvent the wheel. In music, as in science, we build on the work of those who have gone before us. All original composers began with imitation. In borrowing, they developed their craft. Listen to music you enjoy and try to reproduce it on the keyboard. Learn how the music works. This will help imprint the rhythms and structure of effective music into you own hands and brain. Imitation is one of the best ways to learn.

- **Listen.** Listen to yourself and to anyone with whom you're playing.

Track 195

- **Make mistakes.** Don't be afraid to take risks. In a sense, there are no "wrong notes." When you hit a note that seems out of place or clashes with the chord, you can always correct the note and it will sound like it was planned that way. Furthermore, you could even intentionally repeat the mistake and then correct it, making it seem even more like it was planned. Track 195 has a "wrong note" in the second bar. This "wrong note" is repeated in the third bar and then corrected.

- **Hear live performances.** Listen to famous recordings of blues pianists. This will help you internalize the music and rhythm. Also, record yourself playing and determine what areas of your playing need to be improved.

PLAY-ALONG TRACKS

Each play-along track has a four-bar intro and four choruses of the 12-bar blues. The last chorus includes a four-bar blues ending. Each track corresponds to previous tracks in the book, as indicated. Use the licks you've learned and try using the major and minor blues scales in the keys of C and G.

 Track 196

"Barrelhouse Blues." Key of C.
Review Tracks 43 and 49.

 Track 197

"Roadhouse Blues." Key of G.
Review Tracks 60 and 67.

 Track 198

"Back at the Turkey Shack." Key of C.
Review Tracks 80 and 84.

 Track 199

"Lemonade Shuffle." Key of C.
Review Track 92.

 Track 200

"Green Chile Cheeseburger." Key of G.
Review Tracks 99 and 102.

 Track 201

"Jerry B. Fine." Key of C.
Review Tracks 115 and 118.

 Track 202

"ABQ Boogie." Key of C.
Review Tracks 128 and 131.

 Track 203

"Typhoon Tuesday." Key of G.
Review Tracks 137 and 139-141.

 Track 204

"Get Rid of That Stress." Key of C.
Review Track 146.

 Track 205

"Chicken Enchiladas." Key of C Minor.
Review Track 150.

 Track 206

"Gumbo Rhumba." Key of C.
Review Track 160.

 Track 207

"Route 99." Key of G.
Review Tracks 166 and 169.

Track 208

"Jump, Jive and Ginger Ale." Key of G.
Review Tracks 173 and 175.

Todd Lowry   keyboards
John Bartlit   drums
Rodney Bowe   bass

Recorded at Eagle Rock Studios
Albuquerque, New Mexico
Roger Baker, engineer

A BRIEF HISTORY OF BLUES PIANO

Two related styles of African-American piano music – ragtime and blues – arose spontaneously in the American South during the late 1800s. Both styles represented an amalgamation of African and European musical traditions.

Ragtime took its left hand from the "oom-pah, oom-pah" downbeat-upbeat pattern of military marching bands. This pattern later became the basis for the "stride"' piano styles of Fats Waller and James P. Johnson. On top of this stride bass, the ragtime right hand grafted syncopated melodies inspired by African drum rhythms. In fact, the word "ragtime" comes from these "ragged" or syncopated rhythms. The right hand in ragtime generally plays single-note melodies, with occasional octaves, 3rds, or 6ths to thicken the line.

Ragtime was already a viable piano style in 1893, when the classically trained composer Scott Joplin heard it being played at the Chicago World's Fair. He went home to Sedalia, Missouri and began to compose original rags, the first of which was published in 1897. In 1899, Joplin published his "Maple Leaf Rag;" sheet music sales of this and subsequent other rags were incredible. Ragtime became a popular craze from about 1900 to 1917.

Just about every one of the 230 brothels – or "sporting houses" – in New Orleans had a pianist (known as a "professor") who played rags, light classics, and often, blues, on the parlor piano. The legendary Jelly Roll Morton began his career as a professor in a sporting house.

Popular composers such as Irving Berlin tried to capitalize on the ragtime craze with songs like "Alexander's Ragtime Band" – which is not a rag at all, since it contains no syncopation. *The Sting*, a popular 1973 film, popularized the style all over again.

Ragtime is usually written for the solo piano. Blues, on the other hand, began as a vocal style among African slaves brought to work in the fields of the American South. The seeds of the blues were the call-and-response pattern of African tribal music, in which a lead singer calls out a musical line and the group responds by repeating the line. The evolution of the blues continued throughout the rural South in the spirituals, work songs, and field hollers sung by African slaves.

Like ragtime, the blues is an amalgamation of African and European musical traditions. It borrows elements of harmony and form from European musical practice, relying on I-IV-V harmony and strophic form. The form of the blues is three lines of lyrics, with the first line being repeated, in a 12-bar sequence. This three-chord, 12-bar chorus is repeated over and over with improvisation.

The African influence is significant in a number of ways: 1) the melody line consists mostly of descending phrases; 2) the scale contains "blue" notes – i.e. flatted 7ths, 5ths, and 3rds; 3) the voice has an improvisatory quality, employing bent notes, glissandos, melismata, and falsetto; 4) there is much polyrhythmic interplay.

The original blues style was primarily a vocal form. Eventually the blues expanded from a purely vocal musical style to instrumental. Early blues musicians were usually self-taught and impoverished, but blessed with imagination and resourcefulness. They often used "found" instruments such as the washboard, kazoo, jug, or slide whistle, or even made their own instruments such as one-stringed guitar-like instruments.

Blues piano styles had their origin in the rough-and-tumble roadside barrelhouses of the railroad, mining, lumber, and turpentine camps of the late 1800s and early 1900s. Barrelhouses were cheap drinking establishments with barrels stacked along the walls for sitting purposes and a dirt floor for dancing. In those days, most such establishments had a beat-up upright piano in the corner. Pianists drifted from town to town looking for a place to play. They would hop a freight train to the next town and look for a barrelhouse. Odds were good that the place would have a splintered upright. Pianists such as Cow Cow Davenport and Memphis Slim began their careers as wandering barrelhouse musicians.

The pianos in those places were subject to constant abuse from patrons, changing humidity, weekend beer baths, and cigarette burns. The musicians, usually self-taught, adapted to the rough audiences and the mechanical limitations of the instruments with remarkable ingenuity, incorporating the limitations of the instruments into the characteristics of the style. Here, pianists had to develop a rhythmic, aggressive style to be heard above the crowds and to keep pace with the rowdy atmosphere. Barrelhouse players didn't tickle the ivories, they smashed them. The trick was to make the piano heard, so the barrelhouse style featured repetitious left-hand patterns and a pounding right hand.

Barrelhouse blues piano was a cruder style than ragtime. Instead of the "stride" left hand, the typical blues left hand consisted of alternating 5ths and 6ths on each beat. In fact, this left hand is still known as the "barrelhouse" style. It is also clear that the early seeds of boogie-woogie piano were sown in the barrelhouses. Most of the early barrelhouse players are long forgotten, having lived fast and died young in an era before recording technology was available. However, when blues pianists began to be recorded in the 1920s, barrelhouse players such as Cow Cow Davenport made some of the earliest recordings.

In 1917, the Secretary of the Navy closed Storyville, the red-light district in New Orleans, throwing hundreds of black musicians out of work. As a result, many moved north up the Mississippi from New Orleans to Memphis, St. Louis, Kansas City, and beyond. Thus we can credit the Secretary of the Navy, at least partially, for the dissemination of blues and jazz in America.

About the same time, Southern blacks began migrating north to urban centers looking for better jobs. Chicago more than doubled its black population between 1910 and 1920. It became the home to such pianists as Jelly Roll Morton, Cow Cow Davenport, Jimmy Yancey, and Pine Top Smith. Blues pianists began to play at rent parties, a fascinating institution that arose in Chicago and other northern urban centers in response to high rents. By charging admission to a party given in his apartment, a tenant was able to raise enough money to keep a roof over his head.

Sometime during this period, barrelhouse morphed into boogie woogie, although early forms of boogie woogie could be heard in the South during the early 1900s. The essence of boogie-woogie style is its blues structure, fast pace, propulsive "eight-to-the-bar" left-hand figures, and free-wheeling, polyrhythmic blues licks in the right hand. The style demanded skillful hand independence. Boogie woogie was popularized by Jimmy Yancey and Pine Top Smith in Chicago and Pete Johnson in Kansas City. Pine Top Smith is generally credited with introducing the term boogie-woogie into widespread use starting in 1929 when he recorded his "Pine Top's Boogie Woogie."

Like the word "jazz," we don't know where the term "boogie woogie" came from. Some scholars think it might be a variation on the African words "bogi" or "buga" that mean "dance" and "drum beat." Cow Cow Davenport thought it came from the urban legends of the "boogie man," since blues was then often considered to be devilish music. In modern parlance, "boogie on down" and "boogie the night away" simply mean to party and dance.

Boogie became a national craze after talent scout and music impresario John Hammond presented the 1938 and 1939 "Spirituals to Swing" concerts at Carnegie Hall in New York. On the bill were boogie-woogie pianists Pete Johnson from Kansas City, and Meade "Lux" Lewis and Albert Ammons, both from Chicago. The boogie-woogie style quickly caught on – not just in blues, but in popular music. Such songs as "Boogie Woogie Bugle Boy" and "Beat Me Daddy, Eight to the Bar" became huge popular hits. The boogie-woogie style became a foundation of the swing and jump blues styles of the 1940s and rockabilly and rock-and-roll of the 1950s. The height of the boogie-woogie craze was from 1939 to the end of World War II.

After the war, blues piano, which had developed in barrelhouses, began to reach increasingly sophisticated audiences – both black and white. The smooth stylist Jay McShann made his name in Kansas City. On the West Coast, jazz-blues pianists such as Nat King Cole, Charles Brown, and Ray Charles became popular with mixed audiences. The West Coast style is sometimes even characterized as "supper club blues" since it featured swing rhythms, sophisticated substitute harmonies, and smooth vocals.

The Chicago blues style, what we generally consider "modern blues," rose in the late 1940s and 1950s. It had its origin in Delta blues with such artists as Muddy Waters and Elmore James. However, as these Delta musicians migrated to Chicago, they found that audiences wanted a louder, faster, bigger sound. One acoustic musician could not fill a club. Thus, the acoustic guitar was replaced by an electric guitar. Bass, drums, piano, and blues harp usually filled out the lineup, and this combination became the standard Chicago-style blues group. Memphis Slim achieved much success in Chicago starting in the early 1950s. The Chicago style also saw the rise of the featured instrumentalist as a star. One such musician was Otis Spann, the piano player in Muddy Waters' band who became a star in his own right. Later, Pinetop Perkins replaced Spann as Water's pianist and Perkins also achieved success as a soloist.

Meanwhile, back in New Orleans, the pervasive party atmosphere of the "Big Easy" and the blend of different cultures there – European, African-American, Cajun, and Caribbean – led to a vibrant blues scene. A hip-shaking blues piano style had developed, typified by Professor Longhair, that incorporated a syncopated bass line based in Caribbean rhythms. Fats Domino incorporated the New Orleans style into his mainstream rock-and-roll hits, and Dr. John continues the tradition today as a living encyclopedia of New Orleans piano styles.

In the history of American music, the importance of the blues cannot be overestimated. The 12-bar blues is *the* primal structure in American popular music. Because it encompasses the human condition, blues music is timeless. The spirit and flavor of the blues pervade almost all jazz, and its effect can be clearly felt in rock (e.g., Eric Clapton or the Rolling Stones), country (e.g., Hank Williams), R&B, and pop. Although the term "blues" originally connoted melancholy or lament, the affect of blues music is often quite something else. Certainly there are many lament blues in a slow tempo, but the blues is also often played with great rhythmic vitality, and it it's often joyous and life-affirming.

The piano has never occupied as prominent a position in blues as the guitar. Nevertheless, there have been great blues piano virtuosos throughout the decades. See Appendix II for a list.

APPENDIX II
BLUES PIANO PLAYERS

Early Boogie-Woogie Masters

Meade Lux Lewis

Pete Johnson

Pine Top Smith

Cow Cow Davenport

Albert Ammons

Jimmy Yancey

Mississippi Delta School

Sunnyland Slim

Booker T. Laury

Memphis Slim

Piano Red

Mose Allison (a white bluesman from Mississippi with a wry vocal style)

New Orleans School

Jelly Roll Morton (Represents the connection between ragtime and blues. Morton claimed to be the inventor of jazz)

Professor Longhair

Fats Domino (represents the overlap between pop, rhythm and blues and blues)

James Booker (an incredible technician)

Dr. John (Keeper of the flame. A walking encyclopedia of the New Orleans piano tradition.)

Jerry Lee Lewis

Champion Jack Dupree

Chicago School

Jimmy Yancey

Big Maceo

Memphis Slim

Otis Spann (Muddy Waters' pianist)

Pinetop Perkins (Spann's replacement in Muddy Waters' band)

Kansas City School

Count Basie (known for his big band)

Jay McShann

St. Louis School

Roosevelt Sykes

Johnnie Johnson (Chuck Berry's pianist)

Texas School

Marcia Ball (New Orleans-influenced piano style and soulful vocals)

Katie Webster (a fine pianist with a raunchy vocal style)

Moon Mullican

Merril Moore

California School

Nat King Cole (Started as a jazz/ blues piano player. Became famous as a pop crooner.)

Charles Brown (Elegant crooner whose style resembles Nat King Cole)

Amos Milburn

Gospel Blues

Ray Charles

Aretha Franklin (Known as a vocalist, but also a fine pianist)